THE MARVEL'S OF MARCH

MEGHA YADAV

Made with ♥ on the Notion Press Platform
www.notionpress.com

Contents

Contents

CHAPTER ONE

"The Start of Spring: March 1st"

March 1st marks the beginning of the spring season, and with it, the arrival of warmer weather, blooming flowers, and new life. It is a time of renewal and rejuvenation after the long, cold winter.

For many people, March 1st is the perfect opportunity to shake off the winter blues and embrace the new season. This can be done by taking a walk in the park and admiring the budding trees and flowers, planting new seeds in the garden, or simply spending time with friends and family.

For those who live in colder climates, the arrival of spring can be especially exciting. It provides an opportunity to spend more time outdoors and soak up the sun's rays, which can be incredibly uplifting and invigorating.

In many cultures, March 1st is also celebrated as the beginning of the new year. It is a time for new beginnings and fresh starts, and many people choose to mark this occasion by setting new goals or resolutions for the year ahead.

So whether you are welcoming the arrival of spring, setting new goals for the year, or simply enjoying the warmer weather, March 1st is a day to be celebrated and embraced. So get outside, take a walk, and enjoy the start of this wonderful season.

CHAPTER TWO

"Groundhog's Day: March 2nd"

March 2nd is best known for being Groundhog Day, a unique and quirky holiday that has been celebrated in North America for many years. The holiday is based on the belief that if a groundhog sees its shadow on this day, there will be six more weeks of winter. However, if the groundhog does not see its shadow, spring will arrive early.

The most famous groundhog is Punxsutawney Phil, located in Punxsutawney, Pennsylvania. Every year, on Groundhog Day, thousands of people gather to see if Phil will see his shadow or not. This event is broadcasted on national television and has become a beloved tradition for many.

Aside from the fun and excitement of Groundhog Day, the holiday also serves as a reminder of the changing seasons and the cycle of nature. The arrival of spring is an important time for many people, as it marks a new beginning and the end of the winter months.

Whether you are a believer in the groundhog's predictions or simply enjoy the festivities, Groundhog Day is a fun and unique holiday that is worth celebrating. So get out and join in the fun on March 2nd, and let's see what

Punxsutawney Phil has in store for us this year!

CHAPTER THREE

Saint David's Day: March 3rd"

March 3rd is a significant day for the Welsh people, as it is the feast day of Saint David, the patron saint of Wales. Saint David was a 6th-century monk and bishop who is remembered for his wisdom, miracles, and leadership in spreading the Christian faith throughout Wales.

Saint David's Day is celebrated with a range of traditional festivities, including music, dance, and food. One of the most recognizable symbols of the day is the daffodil, which is worn on lapels or hats as a sign of Welsh pride.

In Welsh communities across the world, Saint David's Day is a time to come together and celebrate Welsh culture and heritage. It is an opportunity to reflect on the rich history and traditions of Wales, and to appreciate the contributions that the Welsh people have made to the world.

Whether you are Welsh or simply admire the culture and heritage of Wales, Saint David's Day is a day worth celebrating. So put on your daffodil, join in the festivities, and raise a glass to the patron saint of Wales on March 3rd!

CHAPTER FOUR

"National Grammar Day: March 4th"

March 4th is National Grammar Day, a day dedicated to celebrating the English language and the rules that govern it. This holiday was established to encourage people to pay closer attention to the way they write and speak, and to improve their overall communication skills.

For many people, grammar is an important aspect of their professional and personal lives. Whether you are writing a report, sending an email, or simply having a conversation with friends and family, good grammar can make all the difference.

National Grammar Day is an opportunity to brush up on your grammar skills, and to reflect on the importance of clear and effective communication. It is a day to celebrate the English language and to appreciate the complexities that make it so rich and versatile.

So whether you are a seasoned wordsmith or simply looking to improve your communication skills, National Grammar Day is a day worth observing. So take a moment to reflect on your use of language, and celebrate the importance of good grammar on March 4th!

CHAPTER FIVE

"Mardi Gras: March 5th"

March 5th is Mardi Gras, a festival celebrated with great enthusiasm and fanfare in many countries around the world, particularly in the United States, Brazil, and France.

Mardi Gras, which is French for "Fat Tuesday," is a celebration that takes place the day before Ash Wednesday and the start of the Lenten season. It is a day of indulgence, where people enjoy rich and decadent foods, dance, and revelry before the restrictions of Lent begin.

The most famous Mardi Gras celebrations take place in New Orleans, Louisiana, where the festival has been a tradition for over 300 years. The city is known for its colorful parades, street parties, and elaborate costumes, and attracts visitors from around the world to participate in the festivities.

Whether you are participating in the lively celebrations in New Orleans or simply observing the holiday in your own way, Mardi Gras is a day to let loose, have fun, and enjoy the good things in life. So grab your masks and beads, and join in the Mardi Gras festivities on March 5th!

CHAPTER SIX

"National Frozen Food Day: March 6th"

March 6th is National Frozen Food Day, a day to celebrate the convenience and versatility of frozen foods. This holiday was established to recognize the significant impact that frozen foods have had on the way we eat and live.

Frozen foods have come a long way since their invention in the 1930s. Today, there is a wide range of frozen foods available, from fruits and vegetables to meals and snacks. They are a convenient and affordable way to enjoy healthy and delicious foods, even when time and resources are limited.

National Frozen Food Day is an opportunity to appreciate the convenience and variety of frozen foods, and to explore new and exciting options. Whether you are a fan of frozen pizzas, ice cream, or veggies, there is something for everyone in the world of frozen foods.

So take a moment to celebrate National Frozen Food Day on March 6th, and appreciate the convenience and variety that frozen foods bring to our lives. Let's give a nod to the little packages that make our lives easier, and enjoy a delicious frozen treat!

CHAPTER SEVEN

"National Be Heard Day: March 7th"

March 7th is National Be Heard Day, a day to encourage individuals to express their opinions, ideas, and perspectives. This holiday was established to remind people of the power and importance of their voice, and to inspire them to use it to make a positive difference in the world.

In a world where everyone is vying for attention and trying to be heard, National Be Heard Day provides a unique opportunity to step back, reflect on what you have to say, and make sure that your voice is heard. Whether you are speaking up in a meeting, writing a blog post, or simply having a conversation with friends and family, your voice is important and deserves to be heard.

National Be Heard Day is a day to celebrate the power of free speech, and to appreciate the diversity of opinions and perspectives that make our world so rich and interesting. So take a moment to reflect on the things that matter to you, and make sure that your voice is heard on March 7th!

CHAPTER EIGHT

"International Women's Day: March 8th"

International Women's Day, celebrated annually on March 8th, is a day to celebrate the achievements and contributions of women throughout history and around the world. It is a day to recognize the ongoing struggle for gender equality and to call for a more equitable and just society for all women.

The history of International Women's Day dates back to the early 20th century, when women's rights activists in Europe and the United States began organizing events to commemorate the day. Over time, the holiday has grown and expanded, becoming a global celebration of women's contributions to society and a day to focus on the ongoing challenges facing women everywhere.

One of the key themes of International Women's Day is the pursuit of gender equality. Despite significant progress in recent decades, women around the world continue to face numerous barriers and obstacles that prevent them from achieving equality with men in areas such as education, employment, and political representation. On this day, we reflect on these challenges and work to find solutions that will help close the gender gap.

Another important aspect of International Women's Day is the celebration of women's contributions to society. Women have made, and continue to make, significant contributions in fields ranging from the arts and sciences to business and politics. On this day, we take time to recognize the achievements of women throughout history, and to inspire future generations of women to reach for their dreams and make a positive impact on the world.

International Women's Day is also a time to reflect on the role that women play in our communities and families. Women are the backbone of many societies, taking on numerous responsibilities and roles that help support and sustain their families and communities. On this day, we recognize the important contributions that women make, and we work to create a society that values and respects women's contributions in all areas of life.

Finally, International Women's Day is a time for action. It is a day to call for real, meaningful change that will help advance the cause of gender equality and empower women everywhere. Whether through activism, volunteering, or simply speaking out about the issues that matter, we must all take action to ensure that women have the same opportunities and rights as men, and that their voices are heard and valued in all areas of society.

In conclusion, International Women's Day is a day to celebrate the achievements and contributions of women, to recognize the ongoing struggle for gender equality, and to call for action to create a more equitable and just world for women everywhere. So on March 8th, let us celebrate the inspiring women in our lives, and let us work together to create a brighter, more equitable future for all women.

CHAPTER NINE

"National Barbie Day: March 9th"

National Barbie Day is celebrated annually on March 9th, and it is a day to celebrate one of the most iconic toys in the world: Barbie. Since her creation in 1959, Barbie has been a source of inspiration, creativity, and imagination for girls everywhere, and National Barbie Day is a chance to celebrate her enduring impact on popular culture and the toy industry.

Barbie has been a part of the lives of generations of girls, and her impact on popular culture is undeniable. With her many careers, outfits, and accessories, Barbie has encouraged girls to dream big and to imagine all the possibilities that the world has to offer. Whether as a doctor, astronaut, or fashion model, Barbie has shown girls that they can be anything they want to be, and that there are no limits to what they can achieve.

National Barbie Day is also a time to appreciate the creativity and imagination that Barbie inspires in girls. With her many different looks, careers, and adventures, Barbie provides a blank canvas for girls to let their imaginations run wild, and to create their own unique stories and experiences. Whether playing with dolls or creating their own fashion designs, girls are able to use Barbie to explore their own creativity and to express themselves in unique and imaginative ways.

In recent years, Barbie has also become a source of controversy, with some people critiquing her for her appearance and her role in shaping the expectations and aspirations of young girls. However, despite these criticisms, Barbie remains an enduring icon of the toy industry, and a source of inspiration and imagination for girls everywhere.

So on March 9th, let us celebrate National Barbie Day, and let us remember the enduring impact that this iconic toy has had on generations of girls and on popular culture. Whether you are a collector, a fan, or simply someone who remembers playing with Barbie as a child, National Barbie Day is a time to appreciate the creativity, inspiration, and imagination that she has brought into our lives.

CHAPTER TEN

"National Pack Your Lunch Day: March 10th"

National Pack Your Lunch Day is celebrated annually on March 10th, and it is a day to encourage people to bring their own lunch to work or school instead of eating out. This holiday is a way to promote healthy eating habits, reduce food waste, and save money by preparing your own food at home.

Packing your lunch is a great way to take control of what you eat and to ensure that you are getting the right balance of nutrients and vitamins that your body needs. When you pack your own lunch, you have the freedom to choose what you eat, how much you eat, and how you want to present your food. You can make healthy food choices like packed salads, fruits, and vegetables, or you can indulge in your favorite treats in moderation.

In addition to the health benefits of packing your own lunch, it is also a cost-effective way to save money. Eating out can quickly add up, especially if you are eating out for lunch every day. By packing your own lunch, you can save money and have more control over your spending.

National Pack Your Lunch Day is also a great way to reduce food waste. When you pack your own lunch, you can use leftovers from dinner or prepare just the right amount of food for yourself, reducing the amount of food that goes to waste.

So on March 10th, let us celebrate National Pack Your Lunch Day by packing our own lunch. Whether you are at work, school, or on the go, take the time to pack a healthy and delicious meal that you can enjoy wherever you are. And remember, by packing your own lunch, you are taking control of your health, your budget, and the environment.

CHAPTER ELEVEN

"National Johnny Appleseed Day: March 11th"

National Johnny Appleseed Day is celebrated annually on March 11th, and it is a day to honor the life and legacy of one of America's most famous pioneers and folk heroes, John Chapman, better known as Johnny Appleseed.

Johnny Appleseed was born in Massachusetts in 1774 and became a pioneer nurseryman who travelled across the American Midwest planting apple trees. He was known for his love of nature, his simple and ascetic lifestyle, and his kindness to animals and people. He lived a life of adventure, planting apple trees along the frontier and spreading the joy of fresh fruit to communities across the American wilderness.

Johnny Appleseed is remembered as an American folk hero, and his story has been passed down from generation to generation. He is a symbol of the pioneering spirit that helped to build America and the love of nature and the simple life that continues to inspire people today.

National Johnny Appleseed Day is a time to celebrate his life and legacy and to reflect on the important role that he played in shaping the American landscape. Whether you are an apple lover, a history buff, or simply someone who appreciates the beauty of nature, National Johnny Appleseed Day is a time to celebrate the spirit of adventure and the love of the land that Johnny Appleseed embodied.

So on March 11th, let us celebrate National Johnny Appleseed Day by planting an apple tree, enjoying a slice of apple pie, or simply taking a moment to appreciate the beauty of nature. And let us remember the life and legacy of this American folk hero, who helped to shape the landscape of America and the hearts of the people who call it home.

CHAPTER TWELVE

March 12th: National Plant a Flower Day

It's March 12th, National Plant a Flower Day! Today is the perfect opportunity to celebrate the beauty and joy that flowers bring into our lives. Flowers have been used for centuries to brighten up homes, gardens, and landscapes, and they continue to be a beloved symbol of spring and new beginnings.

Planting flowers can be a fun and rewarding activity for people of all ages. Whether you have a green thumb or are just starting out, planting flowers is a great way to connect with nature and bring some color and life into your home. There are so many different types of flowers to choose from, each with its own unique characteristics and beauty.

If you're new to gardening, start with a small container garden on your windowsill or patio. You can choose from a variety of plants, such as sunflowers, daisies, petunias, or marigolds. These flowers are easy to grow and care for, and they can be enjoyed indoors or outside.

If you have a larger outdoor space, consider planting a flower bed or creating a cutting garden. A flower bed can be a great way to add color and texture to your yard, while a cutting garden allows you to cut fresh flowers for your home or to give as gifts.

No matter how you choose to celebrate National Plant a Flower Day, the important thing is to take some time to appreciate the beauty and wonder of flowers. Whether you're a seasoned gardener or just starting out, there's something truly special about planting and growing flowers. So get your hands dirty, get outside, and plant a flower today!

CHAPTER THIRTEEN

March 13th: National Good Samaritan Day

Today is March 13th, National Good Samaritan Day! This special day is dedicated to recognizing the kindness and generosity of individuals who go out of their way to help others. It is a celebration of the good that exists in the world, and a reminder of the positive impact we can have on others when we act with compassion and empathy.

The concept of the Good Samaritan dates back to biblical times, when a man from the region of Samaria stopped to help a stranger who had been injured and left for dead on the side of the road. The story is told in the Bible as a parable, and it is often cited as an example of how we should treat others with kindness and respect, regardless of their background or circumstances.

National Good Samaritan Day is an opportunity to reflect on the power of kindness and to think about the small actions we can take to make a positive difference in the lives of others. Whether it's helping a neighbor carry groceries, volunteering at a local food bank, or simply holding the door open for someone, every act of kindness has the potential to brighten someone's day and make a positive impact on the world.

So today, on National Good Samaritan Day, take a moment to think about the ways in which you can be a Good Samaritan. Whether you're offering a helping hand or simply spreading joy and positivity, every act of kindness makes a difference. Let's make a commitment to be Good Samaritans all year long!

CHAPTER FOURTEEN

March 14th: Pi Day

March 14th is a day that is celebrated by mathematicians, educators, and math enthusiasts around the world. It's Pi Day! Pi is the symbol used in mathematics to represent the ratio of a circle's circumference to its diameter, and it is an irrational number that goes on forever without repeating. Pi is approximately equal to 3.14, which is why Pi Day is celebrated on March 14th.

Pi Day was first celebrated in 1988 by physicist Larry Shaw at the San Francisco Exploratorium. It quickly gained popularity and has since become a widely recognized holiday, celebrated in schools, universities, and communities around the world.

Pi Day is a great opportunity to learn about and appreciate the importance of mathematics in our lives. It's also a fun way to engage with math and to celebrate the beauty and mystery of numbers. Many schools and organizations hold Pi Day events and contests, such as pie-eating contests, recitation contests, and pi memorization competitions.

If you're looking for a fun and educational way to celebrate Pi Day, consider baking a pie or making a pizza, both of which are circular in shape and can be a fun way to learn about the concept of Pi. You can also spend some time exploring the properties of Pi, such as its infinite decimal representation, or try your hand at solving mathematical puzzles and problems that involve Pi.

So, on this Pi Day, take some time to celebrate the beauty and wonder of mathematics, and to appreciate the role that Pi plays in our lives and in the world around us!

CHAPTER FIFTEEN

March 15th: National Buzzards Day

March 15th marks National Buzzards Day, a day to celebrate one of the most recognizable and iconic birds in North America. The buzzard, also known as the turkey vulture, is a large bird of prey that is found throughout much of the United States and parts of Canada.

Buzzards are known for their distinctive appearance, with their dark feathers and naked heads, as well as their keen sense of smell, which they use to locate carrion, or dead animals. Despite their reputation as scavengers, buzzards play a vital role in maintaining the balance of nature by cleaning up dead animals and recycling nutrients back into the ecosystem.

National Buzzards Day is an opportunity to learn about and appreciate these fascinating birds, as well as to raise awareness about the importance of preserving their habitats and populations.

If you're interested in celebrating National Buzzards Day, consider taking a bird-watching trip to observe buzzards in their natural habitat. You can also support organizations that work to conserve buzzards and their habitats, such as the National Audubon Society or the

Peregrine Fund.

So on this National Buzzards Day, take some time to appreciate the beauty and importance of these fascinating birds, and to learn more about the role they play in our natural world.

CHAPTER SIXTEEN

March 16th: National Everything You Do is Right Day

March 16th is National Everything You Do is Right Day! This special day is a reminder to embrace positivity and self-confidence, and to celebrate all of the things that make us unique and special.

We all have moments when we doubt ourselves, or when we feel like we've made a mistake. But on National Everything You Do is Right Day, we're encouraged to let go of those negative thoughts and to focus on the things that we do well.

This day is a chance to celebrate all of the things that make us special and unique, from our talents and passions to our interests and hobbies. Whether it's cooking, gardening, writing, or playing an instrument, there is something about each of us that is truly special and worth celebrating.

So on this National Everything You Do is Right Day, take some time to reflect on all of the things that make you unique and special. Embrace your strengths, and don't be afraid to take risks and try new things. Everything you do is right, and you have the power to make a positive impact on the world just by being yourself!

CHAPTER SEVENTEEN

March 17th: St. Patrick's Day

March 17th is St. Patrick's Day, a holiday that is celebrated around the world to honor the patron saint of Ireland, Saint Patrick. St. Patrick's Day is a time to celebrate Irish culture and heritage, and it is especially popular in Ireland, where it is a public holiday, and in the United States, where it is widely celebrated by people of Irish descent.

Saint Patrick was a missionary who is said to have converted the Irish people to Christianity in the 5th century. He is known for using the shamrock, a three-leaf clover, to explain the concept of the Holy Trinity to the Irish people.

St. Patrick's Day is a time to celebrate Irish culture and heritage, and it is often marked by parades, parties, and other events. Many people wear green on St. Patrick's Day to show their Irish pride, and some even dye their hair or beards green for the occasion.

The most famous St. Patrick's Day celebration is the St. Patrick's Day Parade in Dublin, which has been held every year since 1931. Other cities around the world also hold St. Patrick's Day parades, and many pubs and restaurants offer special menus and drinks to mark the occasion.

So on this St. Patrick's Day, take some time to celebrate Irish culture and heritage, and to embrace the spirit of this fun and festive holiday. Whether you're Irish or not, St. Patrick's Day is a time to come together and celebrate the things that make life worth living!

CHAPTER EIGHTEEN

March 18th: National Awkward Moments Day

March 18th is National Awkward Moments Day, a day to celebrate the awkward moments that make life interesting and unique. We all have those moments when we feel awkward or embarrassed, but they are often the moments that help us to grow and learn.

Awkward moments can happen to anyone, at any time. Maybe you said the wrong thing, tripped and stumbled in public, or had a moment of social anxiety. But the important thing to remember is that these moments don't define us.

National Awkward Moments Day is a chance to embrace the awkwardness of life, and to recognize that these moments can bring us closer together. When we share our awkward moments with others, we can help to break down the barriers of shame and embarrassment, and we can find common ground with others who have gone through similar experiences.

So on this National Awkward Moments Day, don't be afraid to share your own awkward moments with others. Whether it's with a friend, a family member, or even a stranger, sharing your experiences can help to build stronger connections and to create a more supportive and understanding world.

Embrace the awkward, and let's celebrate all of the moments that make life interesting, unique, and worth living!

CHAPTER NINETEEN

March 19th: National Poultry Day

March 19th is National Poultry Day, a day to celebrate one of the most versatile and widely consumed foods in the world. Poultry, which includes chicken, turkey, and other birds, is a staple in many diets and is used in a variety of dishes, from soups and stews to roasted meats and salads.

Poultry is also an important source of protein, and it is often considered a more healthful alternative to red meat. It is also relatively affordable and widely available, making it a popular choice for families and home cooks.

On National Poultry Day, take some time to appreciate this versatile and delicious food. Try a new poultry recipe, or visit a local farm to learn more about the poultry industry.

Whether you're a fan of roasted chicken, turkey burgers, or spicy chicken wings, there's no denying the popularity and versatility of poultry. So on this National Poultry Day, let's celebrate this delicious food and all of the ways that it makes our lives better!

CHAPTER TWENTY

March 20th: First Day of Spring

March 20th marks the First Day of Spring, a time to celebrate the arrival of warm weather and the end of winter. Spring is a time of renewal and growth, and it is a time to enjoy the beauty of the natural world as the world comes back to life.

The First Day of Spring is celebrated in different ways around the world, but it is often marked by the planting of flowers and the starting of gardens. People take advantage of the warmer weather to get outside and enjoy nature, and they also participate in spring cleaning and other activities that symbolize renewal and growth.

Spring is also a time of rejuvenation and renewal for many people, as they shed the weight of winter and embrace the energy of the new season. Whether it's taking a long walk in the park, enjoying a picnic in the sunshine, or simply taking time to appreciate the beauty of the world around us, spring is a time to celebrate life and all of its wonders.

So on this First Day of Spring, take some time to enjoy the beauty of the world around you. Embrace the renewal and growth of this exciting season, and let the energy and excitement of spring bring new life to your heart and soul.

CHAPTER TWENTY-ONE

March 21st: National Fragrance Day

March 21st is National Fragrance Day, a day to celebrate the sense of smell and the power of fragrance in our lives. Fragrance has the ability to evoke powerful emotions and memories, and it can have a profound impact on our mood and well-being.

On National Fragrance Day, take some time to appreciate the role that fragrance plays in your life. Whether you wear a favorite perfume or cologne, light a scented candle, or simply enjoy the fragrance of fresh flowers, take some time to enjoy the power of scent.

You can also use this day to explore new fragrances and find new scents that bring you joy. Whether you prefer fresh and floral scents, woodsy and earthy fragrances, or spicy and exotic aromas, there's a fragrance out there that is perfect for you.

So on this National Fragrance Day, let's celebrate the power of scent and all of the ways that fragrance makes our lives better. Take some time to explore new fragrances, and let the power of scent bring new joy and happiness into your life!

CHAPTER TWENTY-TWO

March 22nd: National Goof Off Day

March 22nd is National Goof Off Day, a day to set aside your responsibilities and just have some fun. We all lead busy lives, and it can be easy to get caught up in work, school, and other responsibilities. But on National Goof Off Day, it's time to take a break and let yourself relax.

National Goof Off Day is a chance to do something silly, to let your hair down, and to have some fun. Maybe you can try a new hobby, play a silly game, or simply spend some time relaxing with friends and family. The goal is to enjoy yourself and to not take life too seriously.

So on this National Goof Off Day, don't be afraid to be a little silly. Take a break from your responsibilities, and enjoy some much-needed time to relax and have fun. Whether you're a kid or an adult, there's always room for some good-natured fun and play!

CHAPTER TWENTY-THREE

March 23rd: National Chip and Dip Day

March 23rd is National Chip and Dip Day, a day to celebrate one of the most beloved snack foods in the world. Chips and dip are the perfect combination of salty, crunchy, and creamy, and they're a staple at parties, gatherings, and even as an everyday snack.

There are so many different types of chips and dips to choose from, it's hard to know where to start. From classic potato chips and French onion dip, to corn chips and guacamole, to pita chips and hummus, there's a perfect chip and dip pairing for every taste and occasion.

On National Chip and Dip Day, gather your friends and family and enjoy some of your favorite chips and dips. Whether you prefer to enjoy them as a snack, or as a full-fledged meal, chips and dip are the ultimate comfort food.

So on this National Chip and Dip Day, let's celebrate this delicious snack food and all of the fun and memories that it brings to our lives. Grab a bag of chips, a container of your favorite dip, and get ready for a day filled with flavor and fun!

CHAPTER TWENTY-FOUR

March 24th: National Chocolate Covered Raisin Day

March 24th is National Chocolate Covered Raisin Day, a day to celebrate one of the sweetest snack foods out there. Chocolate covered raisins are a classic treat that combines the natural sweetness of raisins with the rich, creamy flavor of chocolate.

These bite-sized treats are perfect for satisfying your sweet tooth, and they're a great option for when you want a sweet snack without the guilt. The raisins provide natural sugar and fiber, while the chocolate adds a touch of indulgence.

On National Chocolate Covered Raisin Day, grab a handful of these delicious treats and enjoy their sweet, satisfying flavor. Whether you prefer dark chocolate or milk chocolate, there's a chocolate covered raisin that's perfect for you.

So on this National Chocolate Covered Raisin Day, let's celebrate this sweet and satisfying snack food. Treat yourself to a bag of chocolate covered raisins, or even try making your own at home. Whatever you do, be sure to enjoy the delicious combination of raisins and chocolate!

CHAPTER TWENTY-FIVE

March 25th: Waffle Day

March 25th is Waffle Day, a day to celebrate one of the most beloved breakfast foods in the world. Waffles are a classic breakfast staple that have been enjoyed for centuries, and they continue to be a popular choice for breakfast, lunch, and even dinner.

Waffles are versatile, delicious, and easy to make, and they can be enjoyed in a variety of ways. Whether you prefer your waffles topped with fresh fruit and syrup, or with bacon and eggs, there's a waffle recipe for everyone.

On Waffle Day, gather your family and friends and enjoy a delicious waffle meal. You can make waffles from scratch, or enjoy a frozen waffle with your favorite toppings. The possibilities are endless!

So on this Waffle Day, let's celebrate this classic breakfast food and all of the memories that it brings to our lives. Grab a hot, fresh waffle and enjoy its crispy, delicious flavor. Happy Waffle Day!

CHAPTER TWENTY-SIX

March 26th: National Spinach Day

March 26th is National Spinach Day, a day to celebrate one of the most nutritious and versatile leafy greens. Spinach is a nutrient-rich food that's packed with vitamins, minerals, and antioxidants, making it an excellent addition to any healthy diet.

Whether you enjoy it raw in a salad, cooked as a side dish, or blended into a smoothie, spinach is a versatile food that can be enjoyed in many different ways. It's also a great source of iron, making it an important food for vegetarians and vegans.

On National Spinach Day, make sure to incorporate this leafy green into your diet in some way. You can try a new spinach recipe, or simply add some fresh spinach to your sandwich or wrap.

So on this National Spinach Day, let's celebrate this nutritious and delicious food and all of the health benefits that it brings to our lives. Grab a handful of spinach and enjoy its crisp, fresh flavor!

CHAPTER TWENTY-SEVEN

March 27th is National Spanish Paella Day, a day to celebrate one of Spain's most famous and beloved dishes. Paella is a traditional Spanish dish that is made with rice, saffron, and a variety of ingredients such as seafood, chicken, and vegetables.

Paella is known for its vibrant yellow color and its rich, flavorful taste. It's a popular dish that's enjoyed by people all over the world, and it's a staple of Spanish cuisine.

On National Spanish Paella Day, gather your friends and family and enjoy a delicious paella meal. You can make paella from scratch, or enjoy a pre-made paella from your favorite restaurant. Either way, you're sure to enjoy the rich, satisfying flavor of this classic Spanish dish.

So on this National Spanish Paella Day, let's celebrate this delicious and flavorful dish and all of the memories that it brings to our lives. Grab a fork and enjoy a steaming hot plate of paella. ¡Buen provecho! (Enjoy your meal!)

CHAPTER TWENTY-EIGHT

March 28th: National Black Forest Cake Day

March 28th is National Black Forest Cake Day, a day to celebrate one of the most beloved and classic desserts in the world. Black Forest Cake is a German cake that is made with layers of chocolate cake, whipped cream, and cherries. It's a rich, indulgent dessert that's sure to satisfy any sweet tooth.

Black Forest Cake is known for its classic combination of chocolate and cherries, and it's a popular dessert that's enjoyed by people all over the world. Whether you prefer a classic version of the cake or a more modern twist, there's a Black Forest Cake recipe out there for everyone.

On National Black Forest Cake Day, gather your friends and family and enjoy a slice (or two) of this classic dessert. You can make a Black Forest Cake from scratch, or order one from your favorite bakery. Either way, you're sure to enjoy the rich, decadent flavor of this classic dessert.

So on this National Black Forest Cake Day, let's celebrate this classic dessert and all of the memories that it brings to our lives. Grab a fork and enjoy a slice (or two) of Black Forest Cake. Happy National Black Forest Cake Day!

CHAPTER TWENTY-NINE

March 29th: National Lemon Chiffon Cake Day

March 29th is National Lemon Chiffon Cake Day, a day to celebrate one of the lightest and freshest cakes in the world. Lemon Chiffon Cake is a light and airy cake that is made with lemon juice and zest, giving it a bright and tangy flavor.

Lemon Chiffon Cake is a popular dessert that's enjoyed by people all over the world, and it's the perfect treat for spring and summer. The light and fluffy texture of the cake, combined with the bright and tangy flavor of the lemon, make it a delicious and refreshing dessert.

On National Lemon Chiffon Cake Day, gather your friends and family and enjoy a slice of this classic dessert. You can make a Lemon Chiffon Cake from scratch, or order one from your favorite bakery. Either way, you're sure to enjoy the bright and tangy flavor of this delicious cake.

So on this National Lemon Chiffon Cake Day, let's celebrate this light and refreshing dessert and all of the memories that it brings to our lives. Grab a fork and enjoy a slice (or two) of Lemon Chiffon Cake. Happy National Lemon Chiffon Cake Day!

CHAPTER THIRTY

March 30th: National Doctors Day

March 30th is National Doctors Day, a day to recognize and celebrate the hard work and dedication of doctors everywhere. Doctors play a crucial role in our health and well-being, and they work tirelessly to diagnose, treat, and care for patients.

National Doctors Day was first established in 1933 by Eudora Brown Almond, a doctor's wife, to honor her husband and all of the other doctors who work so hard to care for their patients. Since then, National Doctors Day has become a nationally recognized holiday, and it's a day to show appreciation for the doctors who work so hard to keep us healthy.

On National Doctors Day, take a moment to thank the doctors in your life. You can send a card, write a letter, or simply say "thank you" to show your appreciation. Doctors play an incredibly important role in our lives, and they deserve our gratitude and recognition.

So on this National Doctors Day, let's celebrate the hard work and dedication of doctors everywhere. Thank you to all of the doctors who work tirelessly to keep us healthy and happy. Happy National Doctors Day!

CHAPTER THIRTY-ONE

March 31st: National Crayon Day

March 31st is National Crayon Day, a day to celebrate one of the most iconic and beloved art supplies in the world. Crayons have been a staple in children's lives for generations, and they have brought countless hours of creative expression and imagination to young artists everywhere.

Crayons are a simple, yet powerful tool that allow us to bring our ideas and imagination to life. They come in a wide range of colors, and they can be used to create anything from abstract masterpieces to realistic portraits.

On National Crayon Day, gather your friends and family and get creative with a box of crayons. You can spend the day coloring, drawing, or simply using crayons to bring your ideas to life. Whether you're a seasoned artist or a beginner, crayons are a fun and easy way to express your creativity.

So on this National Crayon Day, let's celebrate this classic art supply and all of the memories that it brings to our lives. Get out a box of crayons and let your imagination run wild. Happy National Crayon Day!

Printed by Libri Plureos GmbH in Hamburg,
Germany